Praise for JUST BE HONEST

Alexander James is a creative genius that elicits the deepest truths to not only touch the soul but help heal it. The way he weaves pop culture, personal experience, social ills, theology, and truth into a tapestry of hope is incredible. His vulnerability will help bring you to freedom to be who you were created to be.

> —**Tommy Nixon, CEO of Urban Youth Workers Institute**

Alexander James is candid in his collection of poetry *Just Be Honest*. He is courageously honest with himself, his wife, family, church, and community. His pure work will have you checking your own integrity. In his words, he is breaking "generational curses." His guard is down and he has knocked down the walls around his he(art). Praise to James for this brave work.

> —**Jaha Zainabu, Author of *I'm Writing To Tell You***

I didn't know what I was going to get when I read this book of poems from Alexander James. Was it going to be flowery words placed delicately on the page? Was it going to be an amalgamation of metaphors and punchlines that were pleasant to the ears? What I did get was what was mentioned in the title. Honesty. And for that, I was pleased. The way he dove into stories about himself, his family and his past failures were simply refreshing. He had an agenda in mind and that was fulfilled. While reading it, I asked myself, "How truly honest are we with each other?" More importantly, "How honest are we with ourselves?" I appreciate this brother's journey into self-reflection and how he seamlessly did so in the book and ultimately caused you to do the same.

> —**Lem "Saint" Gonsalves, Award-Winning Poet,**
> **Actor and Podcaster**

Alexander James' debut, *Just Be Honest*, dares to boom with a gentle intensity that sears the reader lovingly into thought, introspection, and prayer. *Just Be Honest* is a book of reckoning, reconciliation, and questioning. James questions what it means to be a Black man, a Black son, a Black Father, a Black husband, and a Black man of God. He questions the effects of his upbringing on his present decisions, and he questions the church, but he never questions love. Love is masterfully threaded through this personal narrative with a unique perspective and delightful wordplay. James writes "the father wound/turned tongue and cheek" and this manuscript confronts many wounds, many lies: the ones we were told, the ones we tell others, and the ones we tell ourselves. *Just Be Honest* is not only the title, it is the question James asks of himself of his own life and actions and what he compassionately dares the reader to do as well. James shows us all the blessings that come with honesty, with faith, with love, and with perseverance.

—Siaara Freeman, Poet Laureate
of Cleveland Heights & University Heights

Poignant and pointed, *Just Be Honest* is a vulnerable and honest look at masculinity, fatherhood, Blackness, and faith. Told with a graceful pen of hope that is both illuminating and encouraging.

—S.C. Says, Author of *Golden Brown Skin*

If vulnerability is a secret weapon, then Alexander James is the atom bomb. His audacious, bold storytelling breaks the mold of our idea of poetry as a norm. His words carry illumination from Heaven. His creativity will sear images into your mind fully involving you into the journey of the writer. There is healing, love, and power in all he brings to life. Get ready to go on a ride, but most importantly, get ready to BE HONEST.

—Brandon Allen, Author of *This Little Boy*

Honesty seems to be a hard characteristic to come by these days, but Alexander's work provides an authentic glimpse into his life and thoughts. His poetry is challenging, encouraging, and loving, and his words resonated to my core. Alexander James is a bold, dynamic poet whose words inspire me to be more vulnerable in my own journey as a man and Christ follower.

—Kevin Nickerson, Founder of GameBreakers Academy
& Chaplain for the Los Angeles Rams

Alexander James is an accomplished artist who pierces our hearts and convicts our souls through the fierce beauty of poetry and metaphor. James shows us what it is like to be a Black man, husband, father, son, and Christian in 21st century America by allowing us a glimpse into his innermost being. His honesty is stunning and disarming, and if we listen, we will walk away as better humans for having heard his voice. His *Just Be Honest* collection is courageous and powerful and compels us to confront our racial reality with the hope that we can change.

—Liz Cornell, Racial Reconciliation Advocate

I would have to describe *Just Be Honest* as a collection of suitcases simply because there's so much to unpack. Some of the luggage was good, and some of it was extremely heavy. However, in spite of the heaviness, I felt an overwhelming sense of gratitude. Alexander was not only peeling back the layers and details of his life, but in doing so he allowed us to do the same. Whether it was from the perspective of a father, a son, a Black man, someone overcoming themselves or spiritual forces, someone walking through their faith, or a plethora of topics, it was almost as if he was telling us about ourselves, He himself understands the walk many of us have taken because he himself has been there, and just like many seasoned poets are able to do, Alexander is not only able to give us this body of well crafted, written works, he also causes us to look inward and makes us ask ourselves, "Am I being honest with myself?"

—**Red Lion, Poet**

In a world layered with pain, grief, disappointment, bigotry, and tragedy, Alexander has given us a most loving, beautiful, and hopeful antidote—honesty. Being honest with ourselves and others is the watershed moment for when healing can begin. Alex's prose is not only true, but provides courage for the reader to engage with and walk in truth. And while his writing is undoubtedly brilliant, his greatest artform here is empathy. That is a profound gift to all of us. In reading *Just Be Honest* it occurs to me that perhaps the reason there is a scarcity of honesty these days is because it isn't cheap. It costs something, whether it be our worldview, reasoning, vices, grudges, comforts, or even our pain. That's why I am so grateful for Alex's example of a life that seeks to engage every situation as a fully integrated human being. It is a privilege to call Alexander a good friend, partner in ministry, safe truth teller, and a loving brother, who in many seasons of life now, has helped me carry my burdens and vice versa. This book is a balm for all those who need the beautiful courage and strength to just be honest.

—**Brandon Muchow, Worship Leader**

Alexander brilliantly gives imagery and language to his life story. Each poem slowly and powerfully lures you into a path of self-discovery. Throughout this book, you receive insight into his own pain, trauma, and truth that will not only connect to your experiences but also cause one to wrestle with what was, what is, and most importantly what can be.

—**Vanessa Cruz, Pastor and Youth Advocate**

Some words are big not because they are fancy and require a dictionary to translate. They are big because the emotion they convey and the rhythm they narrate opens corridors into your pain, tenderness and beauty, and mirror prayers you have prayed, verses you have sung, and pictures you have painted in your own heart. You will find those words in *Just Be Honest* by Alexander James.

—Tarabu Betserai Kirkland, Director

Alexander's dedication to the craft and content of poetry really shines through in this new body of work. These are works of art any reader will want to return to often.

—Propaganda, Performing Artist

If life had a manual that painted triumphs and trials with truth intertwined with metaphors, this would be its soundtrack. The transparency and vulnerability that Alexander James utilizes in this book help you to understand how truth can set you free. From cover to cover this book is packed with hard, honest truths. A timely message for this generation.

—Jay O Speaks, Spoken Word Artist

Herein lies Surrender in every poem and Resurrection on every page. A new Gospel, *Just Be Honest*, puts me on trial, elicits true confessions, and has me testifying on my own behalf. It inspires and ignites me to be this excited about honesty, and reminds me that the way out is the way IN. I am redeemed by the good words and works of Alexander James.

—V. Kali, Author of *HYMN*, Facilitator,
Anansi Writers Workshop /
The World Stage Performance Art Gallery

The great actor, singer, and activist Harry Belafonte argued that artists were "the gatekeepers of truth." I am convinced of Belafonte's words, especially as personified in the life, leadership, and work of my brother and colleague in the journey of faith, Alexander James. He is a truth-teller, and his presence and power shine through in the pages of *Just Be Honest.*
Hear them. Weep over them. Celebrate them. Be challenged by them. Be loved by them. Be encouraged by them. And in so doing, join me in honoring our Lord, who has given us this jewel of a vessel: Mr. Alexander James.

—Marcus "Goodie" Goodloe, Ph.D.,
MLKJR Scholar & Leadership Architect

Just
Be
Honest

Just Be Honest

a poetic invitation to liberation

Alexander James

MAMA'S KITCHEN PRESS

Just Be Honest
© 2024, Alexander James
ISBN (paperback): 979-8-9853373-7-2
ISBN (hardcover): 979-8-9853373-8-9

Published by Mama's Kitchen Press
Austin, TX / Los Angeles, CA
mamaskitchenpress.com

First Trade Paperback Original Edition, 2024

Printed in the United States of America

Illustration By Ngima Thogo
Photo by Ashley Nicole
Edited by Anne Marie Wells and Camari Carter Hawkins
Layout Design by Krystle May Statler

To my wife Victoria, my spoon is full of grace.

To my children Theo, Kaleb, Xaiver, and Emmanuel.
You are the greatest poems I will ever write.

To the version of me that I created to keep me safe, thank you.
But I do not need you anymore.

Contents

Preface

If the truth will set you free, what path do lies set you on?

My answer is that lies do not offer a path. They construct a cage, slowly and steadily building on each other until we are a prison constructed by our own choices. To us, our lies protect us, but what began as a suit of armor has now become bolted shut, and we are its prisoners.

I learned through life what Brené Brown once famously said: the opposite of belonging is fitting in. Our culture produces people who read the room and impersonate a version of themselves that will "fit." We are willing to cut off parts of ourselves and leave them behind so we can "fit." The sad thing is how effective the imposter self can be, awarding us with proximity but keeping us from true connection. To belong is the freedom of just being yourself. Being *honest*.

For years I let my fear of rejection from others keep me from ever accepting myself. This book is an escape plan for all those who are tired of auditioning to be themselves. Each poem in this book is a shovel of dirt as I dig toward revelation. This book is a folded note that has been slipped under the bars of your cell asking you to join in on a jailbreak. It is both an initiation and an invitation.

Marriage, Love, Fatherhood, Mental Health, Politics, Faith. This book exposes my honest thoughts on these subjects and more. My hope is that as I tear away at my mask, you find the courage to remove yours as well. However, I must warn you, there is a cost.

People who benefited from your prison will be disappointed by your freedom. Your 9-5 will begin to fund dreams instead of keeping you sleep. Your love life will change because you will love life.

What is waiting for you to…

JUST BE HONEST?

Just Be Honest

Just Be Honest

If the truth will set you free,
then lies build prisons.
Its walls whisper promises of safety and comfort.
But tell me,
If you put flowers and a futon in a fortress,
is it not just a pretty prison?
A spider's web that we weave with our own words?
When a person believes a lie,
there is no need for an ankle bracelet.
Their reflection becomes a warden
for their dreams.
Our lies have a way of becoming a leash.
Each one tethered to a enough truth to give the illusion of freedom.
But just when you begin to flirt with deliverance,
fear yanks us back,
reminds us fear's job is not to give us success, only survival,
revealing that it was never just a prison cell, but a coffin.
Some people call them comfort zones, but I can smell the rotting flesh of
dreams deferred from here.
Comfort zones are graveyards

that hold you, drown you under pillows and preferences.
A thick comforter stuffed with cement and cowardice so you never leave.
It keeps telling you, tomorrow you'll dig out, but it was always a day away.
A paycheck away.
An "if only" away.
Until one day, fear of rejection has buried you.
My wife heard me. Her love called me to freedom.
Her smile was the sunshine waiting for me.
If you are buried under heaps of expectations,
I warn you, don't hide it and settle for comfort.
The truth will set you free.

Deconstruction

Can you honestly say you *know* a thing
that you haven't broken,
that you haven't mishandled,
left shattered in pieces all over the floor?
Can you say
that you know it
inside and out?
If you haven't made a choice
that made its insides come out?

When I was a child, I took things apart.
Curiosity consumed me.
Radios and toys were not safe around me,
but after my hands dismantled a thing,
after my questions carved it open,
I could never get it back to the way it was before.
My goal was not childish destruction,
but mature understanding.

You know a thing thoroughly after you've fractured it,
like how I know my wife's heart so well
because I have broken it,
shattered it into pieces.
I earned every cut on my fingers
as I picked up its pieces,
mended it into a mosaic,
a beautiful pattern of uneven pieces
that has become something altogether new.

We have learned what to do with stains–
make stained glass.
There is intimacy in brokenness.
The willingness to be seen and known
while you are in rubble.

You learn a lot about people in how they
treat you when you are
pebbles.
This is my Deconstruction.
It is to open an investigation
where you are both victim and culprit.
An impassioned interrogation,
with scalpel questions.

It is to pry
principle by principle,
rummage through routines,
claw at my character,
fingering through Faith,
holding myself up to the light,
sustaining third-degree burns on my integrity
asking:
How much of me is edited to the expectations of others?
Has my trauma been a teacher or a tether?

Just like those toys and radios,
when I put myself back together,
I will not be like I was before.
In hopes of living a life that is not
copied and pasted from someone else
because I was too afraid to walk in my own font.
Bold and italicized,
Never again asking
Can I Be Honest?
Because
I will now be,
free from fear.
Just honest.

Just To Survive

Feelings are dangerous
for Black boys.
They are red flags of honesty
while running with the bulls.
Tears make you a target.
We learn organically
to grow callous masks.
Each morning
we audition in front of mirrors,
sagged pants and cracked smiles.
Clench their fist 'til
fingers numb
'cause,
in the hood,
numb is normal.

Every hood has myths and legends.
But when the truth hurts,
you build fantasies to live in.

Most boys are
just following orders from OG's.
Villainous heroes who pass down trauma like
rites of passage 'cause
being a man is the ability to endure.
They jump you into gangs.
This is how you graduate in manliness.
This is how you cross the stage.
Your future brothers surround you.
With knuckles like whetstones
they pummel you until they sculpt you into a stone man.
That's how you earn a name worth remembering—
punches become penmanship.
A check is just a piece of paper
until someone signs it.

And when your brothers pick your body up from the floor,
the hood signs on the dotted line you have worth now.
Men,
with a chest full of C-4,
go out at night
and drink until their fuse is lit.
Go home
and explode
on their children
and their wives
and themselves,
then sleep in the wreckage.
I learned from Peter Pan that the destiny of all lost boys
is to become a pirate.
They trade hands for hooks,
hunt boys who still believe they could fly.
These lies stretch all over the boys' bodies,
convincing them it is a shield,
but surely,
when its mouth closes around them,
it is only a coffin.

Middle Finger

I have asked for forgiveness, often
for the work of my middle finger.
It has cursed more than I could ever bless,
a trumpet of my frustrations,
the crescendo of my bad days,
my baton
used to conduct the symphony of my sarcasm.
But I am convinced
that my son seeks to redeem
my middle finger.
I thought we were just taking a walk.
He treated them as rescue missions.
Whenever we left, he would
seek it out.
His tiny hand would only hold my
middle finger.
He transforms it
into ladder,
to tether,
a bungee cord,
as his feet negotiate with gravity.
He grasps it like a lifeline.
When he stumbles, he squeezes tight,
unintentionally wringing out all the filth
I have dipped it in.
I try to take it back
and offer him other fingers,
but he will not have it.
His tiny soldiers are determined.
They have rejected all but this one.
I do not count it a coincidence
he has chosen
my proudest finger,
humbled it in his grip,

and washed away its spine like
time and waves smooth stone.
I see my finger differently now.
No longer an instrument of war,
just an instrument,
a grappling hook for my son's imagination,
evidence that we are both learning to walk well.
I am not sure if I am holding him up
or
if he is securing me down.
Either way, I am grateful for his grip.

Ringleader

My mother taught me everything
l know about performance.
She was the ringleader of our circus.
When my father decided to be a clown,
pretended to banana peel into destructive habits,
my mother ceased being a target for his pies and apologies.
She packed her troop and moved the tent to a new town.
We were all stuffed in that clown car
the same way we fit in her heart.
My mother taught me to tame lions
built out of pride
or fear.
The way her spine humbled to ask for help when she needed it,
but without losing its strength.
Her spine
had to contort and balance between being
Mother and Father.
She juggled the two roles with elegance
while walking the tightrope of her own womanhood.
She did it all to load her children into a cannon
and light the fuse with night school and Black girl magic.
She blasted us to our destinies.
I am proud to say that I have not come down yet.

Fade

When I take my sons with me to the barbershop,
the other men smirk.
They smile like they got out of doing the dishes,
avoided disaster,
disarmed a bomb that would ruin their day,
and
without fail, one of them says-
"Got you on babysitter duty, huh?"
They all chuckle.
I do not smile.
I inhale slowly,
and I reply,
"No, these are my sons."
They are the reason
I watered all my yesterdays
with sacrifice.
You cannot babysit destiny,
but
I should not be surprised.
Men come here to get something cut off.
Something has grown burdensome,
needs to be trimmed,
and left on the floor
for someone else
to sweep up.
I wonder how many could have grown into fathers,
but decided to fade?
I do not dread being locked up with my children,
whether piggyback or ponytail.
I've chosen to be sown in.
I desire to be the hands
that weave them into
wholeness—
strong enough to be whatever style they desire.

Instead of saying that, though,
I smile.
Today I don't want to argue.
I just want a cut for me and my sons.

A Bad Dude

in response to the shooting of Terence Crutcher

September 16, 2016
Officer Shelby Bo shot and killed Terence Crutcher.
Her husband, upon seeing Terrance from a police helicopter said,
"That looks like a bad dude."

Each morning,
before I leave my home,
I look in the mirror and say:
Remember to smile.
Deflate your chest.
Wave, and make eye contact.
When they see me,
they never see poet,
see father,
see husband.
Their eyes are armed with assumptions and
prejudice makes my skin gunpowder.
The sight of a Black man
breathing
chokes them with fear.
Clinch purse like a newborn,
wait for the next elevator.
No wonder
I must constantly find new ways to disarm myself.
More Carlton less Will.
More CW less BET.
I had to learn quickly to survive.
Compliance is a costume stitched together with
Jim Crow and bias.
Adorned with shackles and chains.
Here, in America,
my biggest threat is being seen as a threat.
I stand vigilant.

Watching how I'm watched.
Interactions with others in the wild
must dwindle into a petting zoo.
Some opportunities, jobs, and stages only come
if I look caged.
I feel like
a dragon who must swallow his flames,
a muzzled shark,
a silent lion.
To survive,
I've made straitjackets
out of your assumptions.
Some days I feel as if
I turned my smile into a white flag,
a way to come across as
"one of the good ones."
I would love to show
the beauty of the
beast in my chest.
How my intelligence can be claw,
be fang,
how I have mastered the bear hug.
But because of my bare skin, most only see
bear skin rug.
My greatest fear is that you will see me or my sons
turning a sidewalk into a runway,
You will be intimidated by
my wings, my freedom.
Prejudice and ignorance
hold hands like
scissors, hungry for feathers,
and to survive,
I will shove myself back into a box,
pay the cost of my tomorrows, so you can feel
superior–
I mean–
safe
today.

All because I want to live,
see my children again,
kiss my wife again.
I pretend that I fit in your boxes
even if it is in a cage of your imagination.
I must be…
a bad dude.

Rest

I want to live how my son sleeps.
My son sleeps like
today was his last day,
and he spent it well.
He sleeps in a peace
that only being empty brings.

He dreams like he poured out all his joy
at the feet of his father.
He smiles like his teeth are retiring after this grin,
like he did everything he wanted to do,
like freedom was his to own.
Today his eyes got drunk on sunshine,
stumbled back into his car-seat throne,
toes tired from shaking hands with every blade of grass,
nostrils full of home.
The grass stains that graffiti his jeans are works of art
designed by choices and not mistakes.

My son sleeps with no anticipation of tomorrow
like a flower bed in the winter that has forgotten about spring.
He is perfectly content with this moment.
He uses each breath to make room for the next.
Mouth gaping open because—
no reason.

Fathers Are First

Some men think they are in the big leagues,
and women are just fastballs they must keep their eyes on.
Their only goal is getting to third base.
While she is trying to pitch, they steal
the idea of home from peewees.
This sets sons on a path of trying
to steal bases for the rest of their life,
positions daughters to swing at every pitch,
unable to read the change up, the curve ball.
Dad was just playing a game,
but it is the children who lose.
Sending them searching for remedies
in beds,
bottles,
bargains,
and bodies.
Fathers break our hearts first, and everyone else
walks on the glass.

Malpractice

It took four years to get J to visit my church.
She called me nervous the night before.
I told her not to worry, just be herself.
She came in the nicest dress she had,
draped in honesty in high heels taller
than her self-esteem.
But,
before she got to her seat,
she was assaulted
by people who thought they were salt.
Eyes like blades cut her down with each step.
Their words were stones.
They drowned her in their opinions.
Asked her to remove her piercings
in the house Jesus purchased with piercings.
She caught eyes with me, threw up the peace,
and walked back out the door.
She never even got the chance to sit.
I have watched shallow people attack others by pulling scripture out of
context like grenade pins.
They grab a single verse and snatch it like loose twine,
unraveling it from its context.
Hold it tightly
just to strangle someone with the string.
Call it ministry,
call it apologetics.
I call it tradition.
These religious folks swim in self-inflicted wounds.
They see the word of God as ammunition,
not medicine.
They use the wood from burned bridges and build thrones,
believing their solitude is a test from God.
When actually…
no one likes them.
These modern-day Pharisees and Scribes are adorned
with church lingo and a pocket full of stones,

but cannot see the Goliath in their shadow.
But humility will come swiftly.
The Holy Spirit will magic carpet the floor from beneath them,
knock them off the beast of their ego.
Doctors have to take an oath that all their
choices are for the good of their patients.
I wonder how many church folks
would have to go to jail
for malpractice.

Cracked

HD finally had enough.
His home had become a pressure cooker,
and he was this close to cracking.
Men know when they are walking on eggshells.
One mistake with the wife and
the argument won't be over easy.
For HD, his sunny side never turned up.
Always too runny.
He felt like he was always running.
But every day, he hid in his shell.
He would cover his face and cheese.
His soft-boiled wife was the only one that did not see
how scrambled he was.
A man can only omelet so much.
I mean fold so much.
I mean hold so much.
He told himself
if you're not at the table, you're on the menu.
Though he worked for the King,
he always felt poached.
The King had money, men and horses.
But they never fixed anything.
HD was convinced
the time for his big break had passed.
His gift was spoiled.
He felt forced into shapes he hated.
No one to open up to,
his thoughts became deviled.
His heart is salty.
What do you expect when you compare yourself
to those who are cage-free?
Until one day,
instead of climbing into bed, he climbed up a wall.
They never found out why he did it.
The official story?
A fall.

The king, his wife, and even the horses were stumped.
But HD knew the truth.
Humpty Dumpty didn't fall.
He jumped.

My Son's Smile

My son, Theo, just turned one.
He does not know the taste of broken promises from his father.
His four teeth are unstained, white,
not decayed from swallowing lies.
Bitterness hasn't ice-picked his teeth jagged.
Cavity-shaped grudges haven't turned his mouth into a bunker,
a foxhole that only opens to fire
to defend itself,
to harm.
When I was young, my tongue was a blacksmith's chisel,
a foundry to weaponize words.
My Father-wound
turned tongue and cheek
into bow and string.
Crazy how not being hugged by your father
makes you want to arm yourself.
How disappointment skips down your root canals,
and blackens every tooth it touches.
My belly, a furnace fueled by brokenness.
My throat, a cursed chimney
bathing my words in black ash.
My smile had many gaps
in my peace,
my joy
my love.
I turned arrogance into braces,
metal and unfeeling,
filled my mouth with rocks,
so my tongue would not be a lonely tombstone.
But now,
for my son,
I must
learn a language other than graveyard.
My faithfulness
to him,
his mother,

his brothers,
myself,
God,
is the best way to ensure his smile is pure.
I pray when he is a man,
If you ever meet him,
I pray he looks at you
in your eyes,
greets you with a warm voice,
shakes your hand.
And…
smiles
like his grin is not weighed down
by his father's faults,
smiles like his cheeks never understood gravity.
Yeah, I pray he smiles.

Resurrection

Depression turns bedrooms into cemeteries,
turns headboards into tombstones.
Blankets become thick soil to bury yourself underneath.
Getting out of bed requires
an excavation.
An archaeological dig to find
A reason to try again.
Once found, we
store it in cold hearts
to refrigerate it
hoping it doesn't spoil.
When you are held by sadness' grip,
every bed is a water bed.
And somehow you are drowning in yourself.
Church folks say just get over it.
You are husband.
You are father.
You are believer.
You are a leader.
But I have learned how quickly titles
can become a tidal wave.
Instead of life rafts,
titles become your life.
And titles are no life at all.
The chip on your
shoulder will become
the stone they roll in front of your
tomb.
But the voice of good friends
becomes the lungs of Christ
calling us out of our own graves.
I have been resurrected by
text messages from thoughtful friends.
You would be amazed how holy
"Thinking about you" can be to
dry souls.

Check on your
"strong friends."
They may need a miracle.
Need a resurrection.

Ashes

My father left well before the divorce.
before the fights,
before stealing.
His disrespect created distance;
an empty shell of a man for at least a year.
Hugs felt hopeful and hollow.
Their marriage was a deflated life raft,
and my mother was out of breath.
They were drifting apart.
And she ran outta try agains.
Fresh outta forgiveness.
So we rowed away one night.
Left my father to drown in his own choices
weighed down by
his demons, his addictions.
To save us, my mother burned the bridge
that led him home.
And now,
twenty-three years later
I stand here at the shore
of that burned bridge
surrounded by the debris
from unfulfilled dreams,
broken promises, and
wasted chances,
the sand decorated with blackened wood.
All the things I wished he would
do
be
teach
provide
protect.
But,
he is still my father,
and without him I have learned to swim.
So, I dive into the charcoaled abyss.

The ashes of what once was
sting my eyes.
So, I shut them tight.
So, I must follow my heart.
Addiction separated us,
but I want to see if that man has found himself.
If he has,
I could better understand
what I have found in me:
this passion
these habits
this appetite
this tongue.
this dissatisfaction
So, I persist
Wading through a moat of his own making,
hoping to find him on the other side.
If I find him, we may never repair the bridge,
but we could still use the pieces.
Hopefully, a bonfire will be enough.
So, as I reach the shore,
shake off the bitterness,
I call out nervously,
Dad, are you still here?

Take My Name

It took my wife two and a half years to legally change her last name.
And for every second after our wedding
that she did not tattoo my name on her identity,
I was bitter.
I felt like escrow never closed on our I do's.
We were married,
but
whenever her job called asking for Mrs. Johnson,
I felt nails dragging over the chalkboard of my peace.
I realize now
what I asked for
was more than whiteout and ink.
When you ask your wife to take your name,
your love is also commanding her
to forget her old one.
You are asking her ears to amnesia
the greeting they are used to.
To become a person she has never been.
To cut ties with the identity that brought you to her
in the first place.
It is not an easy thing
to be baptized under the waters of
a new family name.
You are asking her to evacuate a world that has provided for her needs.
You are asking her to leave the family she has known since breath.
To blast off to a new planet with a hammer, nails, and faith.
It is telling her, that the name she answered to, up until your wedding,
was merely an astronaut suit.
You must convince her to remove her uniform.
Daring her to trust that your love
and grace
and patience
is enough air for the person underneath.
It is a heavy thing.
I see now why my wife took years to change her name.
It was my fault.

I never proved to her that my name
could be embrace
a shield
a pillow
be peace
warmth
provision
that my name was
not a brand on her skin
nor crown of thorns
but holy hieroglyphics.
Victoria, I am sorry
for making my name a task
and not a blanket.
But I am grateful
that we are Jameses.
I will make that mean something.

What If I Have a Girl?

When we found out we were having a son,
I immediately thought of all the things he could get into.
I could smell the grass stains,
see myself buying Band-Aids.
I could already feel his accomplishments swell my pride pregnant.
My wife now says she wants a girl,
and all I can think of is not what we could get into
but
what can get into her.
Or who.
She will be smart, funny, and gorgeous like her mother.
And then
someone will plant lies like seeds in the soil of her self-image.
People eventually will judge her based on her looks,
tell her she is not enough,
that she is just a cup to fill,
that being in a relationship is like a receipt that proves her worth.
Someone will position themselves as Picasso and try to change
the art of her heart.
I know this because
I still have dry paint on my hands from lies I brushed on women.
I am most afraid she will meet someone like who I used to be.
I know
daughters are gifts, not revenge for past sins.
daughters are gifts, not revenge for past sins.
And with all the memorized scripture I have,
If I am honest,
I was...I am afraid.

Enough

There are days in which I feel like I cheated you.
When we exchanged I do's,
we leapfrogged into each other's worlds,
parkoured into each other's hearts.
I sometimes feel that this was not a fair trade.

You gave your hand,
your love, and your faith.
I feel like I gave you my weight.
Along with the ring,
I gave you kettlebells filled with "I can't,"
dumbbells of doubt.

There are days when I believe
it looked like I proposed
on one knee.
But in all honesty,
the weight of this world threw out my back.
When I tried to stand again
and looked up, you were there.
You helped me stand,
helped me heal.
Your love lifted me
You gave me hugs.

And there are days when I feel I just gave you gravity,
like I'm holding you back.
You tell me that's how slingshots work.
I never thought my good thing could also be a Goliath-aimed stone.
I never thought your eyes could be a Crimson Cord to save me from
the war within.
It is easy to love Superman.
But you love the dark Clark in me.
When I am my own wrecking ball,
you are glue.
You know, that white, sticky glue with the cow on it, like from school.

And our sons are popsicle sticks. You work together to reconstruct me.
You have Willy Wonka'd the walls of my heart.
My life is sweeter now.
I feel like I give you reason to pray and give you reason to trust God.

Too often I feel like the thorn in your side.
And maybe that is my place: in your side.
It just doesn't seem fair to me sometimes
like kids trading lunches, I feel like
you got a cheese sandwich
and I got a pizza Lunchable with a Crunch bar.

You have been both pillow and pillar.
Your honesty honed me in honorable.
You tell me I am enough, and
I am trying to believe you.
But I often feel like I am not enough.

Men Where I'm From

Men seem to treat expectation
like a virus.
So, they prescribe themselves over-the-counter liquor–
an attempt to drown this flu of accountability,
quarantine themselves in clubs, and porches.
They see homes as anchors on their joy,
family is feared as a threat to freedom.
I have watched the promises of man quicksand at the sight of expectation.
Men whose word dissolves as fast as witches in water.
They should not fold as quickly as taco shells when the heat is raised.
How can they ever hold the weight of a wife or family
if their arms are strong but their hearts are brittle?
A man is only as good as his word.
Ask yourself:
If you were a man of your word,
would you even exist?

Light

It is not the darkness that scares me.
It's how much being a light burns.

Holding My Breath

I will never forget when I started to swim in the deep end of the Bible.
I was sitting in the kitchen,
my heart standing on a diving board.
It took me a while to work up the courage to stop trusting my legs,
to let gravity and God bear the weight of my questions.
I would dive in head first
searching for a truth that would fit in my pocket,
looking for God to come along and highlight my already conceived notions.
But I learned that until we abandon what we think we know,
we will never submerge.
Our opinions are like water wings:
they will never let you plummet into God's promises.
That might explain the believers who have only gotten their feet wet.
Until you kamikaze your sandcastle, you will never be wiped clean by the wave of his wisdom.
You will just float.
Your comforts will creep up like mainsail,
and every wind and doctrine will make you drift.
How many believers do you know who ride comfortably
on a raft built out of their parents' prayers?
Those who have no desire to truly know him?
This explains why many churches are just kiddie pools.
Why so many believers' walk with God is
so slip-and-slide.
I was there.
Then I saw a man.
No life vests.
He said my life was not my own.
No water wings.
He flipped pages like the breast strokes.
Humble.
Doggy paddled through text like he savored every syllable.
Sometimes, he would just be still and let it wash over him.
He treated each chapter like Noah. He believed that it would rain down on him. But instead, he was working to dismantle his ark of convenience.

For the first time I said,
I want to know you like that.
That man is my pastor. Pastor Jones.
He has been my lifeguard ever since.
Now when I read the Bible,
I open my mind & heart
and hold my breath.

Too Woke

Videos of Black death on Facebook was all the algorithm
showed me for weeks. So, I decided not to watch any more.
I would shelter my energy from another pain.
But when I would scroll past another execution,
I felt guilty.
All I can think of is Emmett Till's mother
choosing an open casket.
There is a collective trauma that we carry,
and I feel like I'm letting my folks down
not holding up my end of the bargain
if I avert my eyes.

To be Black is to be forced
into being forever a pallbearer,
to be invited to a funeral that never ends,
to watch mothers never take off their veil,
every Sunday a repast
I do not need another apology
or another eulogy.
Just a break.
I have learned you
can not be so Woke
that you can't sleep.
Pray for me.

Pride

I was told that the path to humility
was in swallowing my pride,
but they forgot to tell me
that you are what you eat.

Jones

Last Sunday,
like it was the first time,
I looked at my Pastor.
Forehead wrinkled like the hallway of a library
stored with knowledge for the willing.
His vision sees potential when others only see problems.
A voice like a mix between Uncle Phil and King Solomon.
A laugh that bellows
A whisper like telling lullabies to lions,
eyes that see you whole.
His eyes are a nest:
you can rest there, but
they are also used as crow's feet.
Ears like satellites having to constantly receive multiple signals and process.
A heart that ignores pain to feed passion.
Hands scarred from sheep bites.
One who fights wolves while we sleep by still waters.
Pastors have such a unique job description:
A sheep that has taught itself to stand on its hind legs and mimic its
shepherd,
given staff and rod like a child wearing their father's shoes.
And at moments, I could imagine it still feels like dress up to him.
King and peasant blended like hot and cold air;
a beautiful mix of change and pain.
No wonder sermons are hurricanes for the dry gardens of our souls.
So next time, take some time and look at your pastor
what do you see?

Living Room

Theo always runs down our hallway.
His two-year-old feet high-fiving the wood floor.
Each step
sweet and careless.
The sound of his joyous toes
drown out the creaks with jubilee.
The thump of his heel
is healing.

Thump thump thump thump

His footsteps have become
the heartbeat of our house.

When you touch the doorknob,
I promise,
you can feel it.
You can feel the pulse of our family,
warm
and inviting.
His laughter is its lungs.
His joy keeps us breathing,
keeps us living
and
we are alive as well.

I listen to my wife, sometimes.

Whenever my wife critiques me,
I listen.
But
if it counters my own paper-mache gospel,
if it opposes my elbow-greased ego,
my earned holiness,
if it does not shine my golden calf muscles,
if she attempts to be wind of truth
to my careful house of cards,
if her love grows her horns
and turns her bull in the china shop of my pride,
if her honesty pokes the eyes out of my peacock feathers,
I do not listen.

I make her heretic.
Her perspective and truth turn her to Pharisee and scribe.
I treat her to the brood of vipers in my tongue.
My critiques of her lash out
like whips for her sin of having expectations,
as if proving there is poison in her well somehow purifies my own.
The problem is, she knows.
She knows many of my relationships are veiled sanctuaries
inviting you to my performance of who I think you want me to be.
But she refuses.
My lies are yellow brick roads to her.
She is the Dorothy that is unafraid
of the mechanized masculinity.
She sees the man past the singing scarecrow,
past roaring lion,
she is determined to transplant heart into this tin man.
Her love is oil for my rusted parts.
She patiently takes my hand,
gives me the courage
to drop my fig leaves.
They dance to the floor
on a staircase of wind

with my worries,
with my anxieties.
My wife's critiques are more construction
than I ever give her credit for.
I should listen.

Good Religion

Has the weight of someone else's situation
ever hung your head low?
Has someone else's fate ever tiptoed up your spine,
dressing your mind in hand-me-down fear?
When was the last time sadness
stepped on your throat?
Has your heart ever been broken
because someone else's stopped?
We are called to be brothers and sisters.
A family lineage that stretches back to a picnic in Eden.
I fear that we have glorified joy.
But not true joy.
A joy that is watered by others' pain.
A happy that it is not at our house,
our family,
our wallets.
I am just asking you
to interrogate your holy.
Would you stand in the way of harm meant for someone else?
Would you be willing to soften the blow with your body?
Would you let your ear become body bag
so some can work through their grief?
Would you let their bloody knuckle punches
decorate the wallpaper of your free time?
I am often terrified
at what the church is becoming:
a mechanical brute that dredges forth.
A distracted guardian
walking past the wounded
on its way to church.
I'm pretty sure the point of this was to be Jesus's body.
Where are the hands?
Where are the feet taking us?
When was the last time you could see the check engine lights in their eyes?
The last time you popped the hood?
When have you asked,

"No, for real, how are you?"
and allowed yourself to be a tool used by a masterful mechanic?
Now, more than ever,
Christ needs a body to work through.
But
maybe you are still caressing your own wounds,
fearful of hugging with broken arms.
I get that.
But we must remember
that Christ holds us.
His hands have scars shaped like sacrifice,
his love chased us with feet punctured by purpose.
So, we can be hurt and still heal.
So, ask yourself.
If you don't give of your body,
what good is your religion?

Hood Prophecies

My sons hear the same prophecies I did.
"He's gonna be strong"
NBA
NFL
You see,
when the Deacons of the hood
lay hands on you
to anoint you with purpose,
they also attach a bungee cord to your passion.
Tattoo a Jordan jumpman on your
eyelids.
I learned young not to color
or
dream out of the field goal lines.
To keep spoken desires
in bounds.
All my fantasies had to be for football leagues.
It's terrifying how quick basketball courts turn into the coffins
for Black boys' imagination.
Because if you don't play sports as a Black boy...
your height
your weight
your body
is a waste.
Men constantly say what they would do in your body.
Women whisper what they would do to your body.
When you are a big Black boy,
your body is ammo for others' imagination.

In the hood,
melanin is a uniform.
I wonder how many pharmacy technicians
are being restrained in a practice jersey right now?
But
stereotypes will not jail my sons.
My sons are big for their age.

Broad shoulders.
But what if they are for holding up the weight of their friends' burdens?
Their feet are big.
What if that's so they leave a trail behind themselves like their father did?
They are tall for their age.
But what if that is so they can reach the cereal for their r grandmother?
While their hearts are still Play-Doh
I will not let people
tell them what shape to make.
I can see them stiff-arm imposter syndrome
to touch down
in their wives' hearts.
I can see them carrying generations,
not footballs.

Fit the Description

I have worn a size 15 shoe
since seventh grade.
This means that shoe shopping has never been fun for me.
I remember the day when I no longer fit shirts from Target.
I got an F in PE in high school, twice.
It was my first period, and they refused to give me larger shorts.
My mother did the best she could, but
I didn't have jeans that really fit me until I was 17.
I was raised never really knowing what fit felt like.
Now I understand.
I'm a big black boy.
Things were not constructed with my consideration
other than my containment.
To most, the only thing I would ever fit
is the description.
I remember being stopped by police officers on my walks home.
They looked at me like prison orange was just my size.
Stretched me out like a tailor over squad cars.
Trying to find what they could make fit.
Measured my worth.
Squeezed me inside squad cars like tight jeans.
Too many innocent men have been buttoned-up with tidy knockoff
convictions.
And when I ask them why.
They always say the same thing:
"Well, Sir, you fit the description."

Flinch

My wife told me today,
When you reach for your sons, they don't flinch.
There is no fear in their eyes.
No second thought.
When I reach for my boys, they don't prepare to fight.
They open up like a lonely, buried treasure
and my arms are shovels.
They reach back confident in the arms that have held them so much and
so often.
Arms that their imagination has molded into ladders.
Jet packs to escape with.
My hope is that these arms would be
rod and staff to them.
Both guide and guardian.
The more I find out about the history of men in my family,
the more miracle it is to me that
I am a safe place for my sons.
When I reach for my boys, they don't prepare to fight,
to defend themselves,
to prove something.
My wife said,
When you reach for your boys, they don't flinch.
Yes, this is a generational curse
breaking.

The Talk

Every Black parent knows that for their children,
growth spurts are bittersweet.
Your excitement for the stretch of your child's legs,
how every inch they grow brings with it a measure of terror.
When black parents watch their children's bodies build,
they worry
because we know as they begin to twin tower,
someone's 911 call
becomes your 9/11.
So, you have to have the talk.
And to be quite honest with you,
I'm sick of it.
I have a different question -
White parents, have y'all had the talk yet?
Have you told your sons not to become monsters?
Taught your daughters not to weaponize their tears?
That the absence of melanin does not make one more moral?
After the birds and the bees,
tell them about the bodies in the trees.
After puberty and what their minds can do,
tell them about the strange fruit.
When black birds flocked to build nests in Tulsa
and someone's son
burned it to the ground,
how many people would still be here if they weren't stung
leaving their queens to raise gardens alone?
If I have to talk to my son,
you should have to talk to yours.
We are all the ingredients that were poured in.
Aren't we?
My children will be judged by the deeds of the few.
But white children are spoken about
like comrades and never columbines
when mass shooters across the country
could share IDs.
If I have to tell my children that they will be viewed as less than human,

teach your children to hold onto their own humanity.
If I have to tell my children
that they were born with a target painted on their backs,
you should teach your children to put down the paint brushes.

I understand that you want children to have a healthy self-image,
to view themselves as kings and queens
but let us also ask ourselves,
who are we telling them are their subjects?
Who are we teaching them that they reign over?
Ending racism is not just about the strength of Black dignity.
It is also disarming the eyes that would see them as a threat in the first
place.
We all need to have the talk.

Insurrection

"I Pledge allegiance"
I would walk to school with my siblings every morning,
bundled in warm clothes like somebody loved me.
Only thing exposed were my Hershey cheeks.
They would get kissed by chilly LA mornings with every breeze.
When we would get to school,
they always started the same way.
We would stand on dots on the gravel playground.
We were told to look up, face the flag.
"To the flag"
They would make me take my
little black hand and
put it over my little black heart,
say with my little black tongue
the pledge of allegiance.
"with liberty"
Looking back on it now, I'm furious.
Isn't it crazy how they made young kids repeat the Pledge of Allegiance
to a country that never intended on keeping its promise to them?
They told us to love our country,
respect the laws of our country,
join the military fight and die for our country.
They act as if there isn't a moment where my little black hand
isn't little anymore,
where they make my whole body a big black weapon.
"And justice…"
And then on January 6, 2020,
they stormed the capital of the country
that they told me to pledge allegiance to.
They attacked the police that they told me
I should listen to and respect.
They smeared feces on the wall
like the monkeys that they called me.
Held the flag they told me not to disregard
and used it to beat guards.
"For All"

The people who told Kaepernick not to kneel
stomped privileged feet on Capitol Police.
They built gallows to hang the vice president but
called me unpatriotic for having expectations for my country.
Funny, they lost one election
and misplaced their minds.
They felt minority for one moment and revolted.
The same coverage that called them passionate
called me thug for less.
I am starting to think those who hold
this country accountable
are the true patriots.

Choir Auditions

I figured it out.
God just needed another black choir in Heaven.
Sandra Bland is the best alto he's had in years.
Tanisha Anderson,
Korryn Gaines,
and
Miriam Carey are tearing up that soprano note.
Tamir Rice was so young his voice never dropped.
He is probably hitting that soprano note like
Westley from Sister Act 2.
And the tenor section must be incredible for Philando Castile,
Michael Brown,
Freddie Gray.
And you know who the choir director is? Botham Jean.
I can hear them now
"Oh When The Saints Go Marching In…"

Encourage

Can you tell someone who did not have a good night
"Good morning"?
Will your smile and syllables
be enough to change the astrology of their heart,
move the moon?
Can you become wishing star
in the phantom of their sky,
redirect the gravity of their grin?
What if they have seen too many stars spill out of Heaven
and their wishes crash with them?
People who get visits from depression notice who stops calling.
They detect the difference between people who are willing
to mourn with them.
Those who are willing to orbit, and just share space when words fail.
Unknowingly turn into an asteroid belt that holds the person up.
Decorates their universe with friendship.
When sorrow is a black hole that has robbed the planet of air,
these people hold their breath and their friends.
But then there are those who only seek to be Halley's comet.
Beautiful, but only for a moment.
No desire to be the sun or moon but a strobe light of encouragement.
Those that tell you how your sadness affects them.
Acts as if sadness is a matter of strength.
They attempt to rain down assurance without realizing
they've become a dark cloud themselves.
I have learned that my best friends treat me as if I am a star
that they will not let fall.
And the best way to serve a star is to just simply be the black sky
that holds it up,
drawing no attention to yourself.
Serving the purpose of making the star look brighter.
Some people need space.
Some need you to be space.

Nerf

The commercials were life-changing.
Each ended with a declaration of foam war
with a child holding a toy gun twice his size.
It's Nerf or nothing.
And I would watch eyes glazed over imagining myself
Rambo
Shaft
Neo from The Matrix
I would answer the call of duty and rock my halo tilted.
I was a child who wanted to play with guns.
However, I was also young
and Black in America,
and this fact had already disarmed my mother
from any idea of us playing with toy guns.
You see, a Black mother can detect the Tamir Rice in her son.
That's when I realized, when the commercial came on
the boys in it did not look like me
leaping around barriers
shooting around corners
reloading with excitement in their hearts.
They would say, "It's Nerf or nothing!"
I will always assume that for me and boys who looks like me
it must be
Nothing.
Because police don't use Nerf guns.

Pirates of the Playground

My son and I have sailed oceans of astro turf,
battled through rusted jungles,
jousted dragons armed with toy swords and strollers.
Ours is a bond built by bruises,
thickened like scabs in the summer.
Painful, but worth it.
We are infamous from LA to Long Beach.
We have dueled thousands of blades
of grass with just our toes.
We have tamed many forgotten slides,
places that are only cleaned
when clouds purge.
But we give those puddles left behind purpose.
We cannonball into them.
We have found treasure in places that the city governor's budget has
abandoned.
We have become each other's compass.
Pirates of the playground.
We have found the treasure
in each other's chest.
We have decided for as long as we can,
each breath will be an adventure.

My Wife's Body

My wife's body is not a reward for singleness time served,
for taking out the trash,
for doing dishes, or
fixing the vacuum.
It is a treasure stored in the part of Heaven I can reach,
a pool of Bethesda I can bathe in.
My wife's body is not payment
for completing a mile-long honey do list.
It is a marathon whose every curve I don't deserve.
My wife's body is not a workshop
for me to spend hours in, trying to build an identity.
It is a reflection of God's grace.
My wife's body is not a finish line
where my heart and mind turn tortoise and hare, racing to prove something.
It is a fountain of wisdom I get to sip.
My wife's body is not a reservoir
of things I like to hear.
Her throat is not a well that I throw money at to wish her silent.
My wife's body is not recycle bin
where I deposit my broken
and she gives me value.
It is not her job to make me whole;
Jesus does that.
I asked God about my wife's body.
He told me she has never been re-made,
that He is out of stock of her
mile,
that she had a body before she was my wife,
that she was crafted as carefully as constellations,
She has been a candle burning for God prior to her lighting
my path with her brilliance.
And I would not trade my wife's body
for anybody.

Faith

Sometimes
we must stare into the eyes of our Goliath
and not blink,
put both hands on the helm as we head into a storm
and not turn,
tell the king before being thrown into the furnace,
My choice has been made.
When our anchorless hearts are
adrift in a storm of tears,
we must stop looking for a lighthouse
and remember
this little light of mine is enough.
Though our bodies may be fractured,
shattered on the shores suffering,
when the wedding is out of wine,
when your past mounts chariots and chases you down,
remember that you have tasted the liberty of his love,
your eyes have peered into promised land only to find a person
who offers home to soul refugees.

After our dying breath has hurdled over our lips,
our final gasp,
our last morsel of might,
we will whisper
these words:
"The Lord Is My Shepherd"

July 4th, 2018

Somewhere there is Manuel,
Eight years old, 60 pounds.
A small boy.
You can barely make out his thin figure during flashes of light from the
fireworks that he saw through the window.
Chain link shadows tattoo his skin with each explosion of color and light,
covering him with X's
as if to cross out his American dreams
before they breathed diplomacy.
Manuel came to America following his father,
but
when they hopscotched over America's imaginary line,
they could not hop back.
They put him and his father in
separate cars,
separate teams,
separate states.
They have been playing hide-and-seek ever since.
Manuel does not want to play anymore.
He stands there wishing he was not so good at hiding
so his father could find him.
He just wanted to taste American cherry pie.
He sees a bright red firework.
In another state,
there is Maria,
42.
She can see the fireworks
from the backseat of the truck
she was thrown in.
Her arms burn where her daughter's nails dug trenches
in her wrist as ICE agents pulled them they pulled them apart.
The cramp in her leg screamed to be repositioned,
but the men in the truck didn't speak her language.
The scratches from the high weeds had kissed her ankles deeply,
left its lipstick up and down her body.
She is seated between two guards who smell of privilege.

She remembers she promised her daughter they would try cherry pie.
She sees bright red fireworks.
And then, somewhere,
there is Susan or Karen or Nancy.
She tightens her apron before pulling the cherry pie out of the oven.
She can hear her son's footsteps rush down the stairs
in response to the aroma.
Her son pulls her hand outside of their Texas home
to watch fireworks as the pie cools.
Dad is cannonballing in the pool
just to splash them both.
They giggle.
The father complains, "Cherry pie, again!"
And they look up at a bright red firework that dances over the pool water.
All three of these stories happen in the same country.
Under the same sky, on the same night.
This is America.

My Apologies

I have to apologize to you all
because whenever I hear your names:
Trayvon Martin
Freddie Gray
Philando Castile
Terence Crutcher
Sandra Bland
Alton Sterling
Natasha McKenna
Tamir Rice
Michael Brown
Eric Garner
Tyre Nichols
My train of thought hits a landmine.
My veins flood with gasoline.
And every new name is a lit match
I am forced to swallow.
I have run out of tears.
Only indignation.
This pain has ripped me apart now.
I am held together with hashtags.
#blacklivesmatter
But, I can't let myself be consumed in rage
because doing so would be the greatest insult to you,
to all of you.
If your names trigger me,
then I, too, turn you into a weapon,
a reason to throw away the future they took from you.
Not as a person, but justification for destruction,
I will not let your names become weapons.
I pray I get to the place where your names are high-fives and medical bags.
Fertilizer for my dreams.
Alarm clocks that keep me woke.
My prayer is for your families &
to not let me become the monsters
I am trying to defeat.

Pluto

One day,
Pluto woke up,
washed his hands in the Milky Way,
wiped the comets from its eye,
and yawned with galactic morning breath.

Glanced over and looked at Earth,
lovingly,
But his heart landed on hostile territory.
He almost fell out of orbit at what he saw.

In school books,
on posters, and even t-shirts all across the Earth,

"There are only
8 planets now."

He had been deleted,
Received a galactic demotion.

He complained to Neptune,
but all he received was a cold shoulder.

So, Pluto googled it.

"In 2006, a global group of astronomy experts established a definition of a
planet that required it to be the largest gravitational force in its orbit. Since
Neptune's gravity influences Pluto, Pluto was out of planet status."

Pluto doesn't even have oxygen
and found a way to go breathless.

I, too, know this feeling
when people you have never met
in a room you have never been in, decide
what you are,

who you are,
that your body is no longer heavenly,
that because you do not revolve in your own domain,
you are less.
Dwarfed in their presence.

How can I get to infinity and beyond
if the gravity of my blackness is seen as a hole in my resume?
What did I do if since birth
Houston has had a problem
with me?

Funny,
24 billion dollars are budgeted to build ship and sail space

while 80% of Earth's oceans are still undiscovered.
I guess it's easier to share opinions of other people and planets
than to persevere through the pressure of
Pressing deep into your own deep end.

I guess it's easier to grapple with gravity than endure wading in the water

as if we don't orbit the same sun,
as if our children aren't fed
and drink from the same Milky Way.
When Neil Armstrong is kneeling on the neck of your atmosphere,
they take one small step
over you,
then make giant leaps to conclusions.

I have watched people's opinions of me pandemic all around me
until everyone is moonwalking away.

I feel for Pluto because
I have been Pluto,
I am Pluto.

Magic School Bus

What would happen if Ms. Frizzle
took her class on one last field trip?
It would go like...
Today, class, we are going to check out an endangered species.
Which one Ms. Frizzle? Ralphie would say
as they boarded their magic yellow Uber.

Phoebe would say,
Doesn't matter, Ralphie,
Gonna be great!
The class would scamper to their seats,
feet filled with hopeful expectations
as they pulled off from school,
all anticipating the moment of transformation.
The children, so used to yellow,
whirlwind
to become an airplane, pizza, butterfly.
Liz the lizard
would don her red helmet and
give a thumbs up.
The children would wait with baited breath
for that familiar phrase,
the words that prepared them to morph, to change
to become something else, or
someone else.
They would clinch the back of the seats in front of them,
fingertips full of suspense.

Ms. Frizzle would smirk
reach for her magic lever and
say it: "COME ON BUS, DO YOUR STUFF!"
She'd pull it.
The bus would shake.
Spin.
Teleport them through space and time.
Colors would catapult them through constellations

all the way to…
Chicago.
The children's faces would freeze.
The bus would become...a bullet
in the gun of an officer filled with
justification and power.
His finger would pulsate with fear and authority.
The officer would see a dark weapon,
I mean, Black boy.
Ms. Frizzle would tell the class,
Today, we'll learn about the insides of an endangered species:
an African-American in America.

Bang!
The bus, I mean, bullet would fly
through the boy's future and bury him in a hashtag.
Ms. Frizzle would shout, Time to split up!
as the bullet shattered on his collar bone.
GET OUT THERE AND EXPLORE!
The kids would sail his blood stream on fragments.
Ralphie, lodged in the boy's shoulder blade would say,
What is on his throat?
Dorothy would say, It looks like fingerprints.
Frizzle would reply, Yes, from being strangled
by those who told him he had no voice,
told him to shut up and play,
treated his cries as lullabies.
Tim–the black kid on the show–
Would run his fingers over his own throat in a familiar way.
Wanda, whose bullet fragment would be floating down the aorta,
would say - Wow, look at his heart! It is glowing!!!
Frizzle would be like,
Yes,
his heart is special,
regardless of what amount of hate is heaped on it, still
gave
Martin
gave

Malcom
gave
Aretha
Black culture has always been America's recycling bin,
but people taught him his skin was eclipse
so he would never look inside for light.
Kesha would be like,
It's beautiful.
Phoebe and Carlos,
who are in the boy's right and left lungs,
hovering in his last breath,
would say,
Why!
Why!
Can't we stop laughing?
Ms. Frizzle would say,
Oh, now you can let people know there is nothing like
BLACK BOY JOY
A happy not sourced on Earth.
Black boys have joy like a Phoenix;
whenever they're burned,
they can rise up again.
The children would learn a lot that day.
Well, all but one.

Arnold in a bright orange jumpsuit would
lie still in the bus in the fetal position, rocking back and forth,
whispering to himself,
like he always did,
I should have stayed home today,
I should have stayed home today.

Redwoods

The Roman Colosseum.
Machu Picchu.
The Great Wall.
A colossal grinning Jesus.
Earth is adorned with these marvels that drown unprepared hearts in awe.
We call them the Wonders of the World.
People travel from other countries,
hundreds of miles, to see them.
My favorite, however, are the trees,
giant red trees.
The feeling of galloping curious fingers
over scars in their bark.
Toes doing ballet over exposed roots,
witnessing their magnitude.
Makes me happy to feel small.
My favorite thing about Redwoods
is the way they
serenade with chords, convinced
their audience is mother nature's father,
how they dress like they've been through something.
Every Sunday, I proudly become tourist,
watch them show up early…
for church.
Have you ever seen trees park cars?
Get dropped off by their children?
What a wonder.
The elderly members of my church
are my Redwoods.
Rooted in a faith that has been tested like gold before a craftsman.
Did you know some redwoods wear coats of ash
from fires they danced in and survived?
Black skin transformed into jackets of endurance,
sheltering souls too stubborn to burn,
saints who no longer see problems,
just patterns,
treat hurricanes like watering pots in

the hands of a faithful gardener.
They have sprouted a
faith that turns feet into anchors.

You will not always find flawless
theology in them,
but their breath glorifies the Lord in ways
that make mountains jealous.
They have stopped searching for his plan in things
completely content
simply because God is in it.
They are not perfect, but persevered,
mason jars of truth screwed on tight with dignity.
I love to listen to their stories;
their tongues are sewing needles
transforming good food into thread
that stitches families together.
Though they are an endangered species, they exist.
We, millennials, have left them dry and unattended.
We have been missing the forest for the trees,
believing that our ripped jeans
fog lights
viral videos
theology degrees get us closer to God.
Trading faithfulness for fireworks.
But these Redwoods have been watered by a secret fountain
drawn from an ocean of love.
They have no fear of lumberjacks
or axes
or questions
or fire
Growing through every season,
their leaves have transformed
into the color of silver testimonies.
What is it to be held by a faith for 50 years
and decide not to become statues in the park
but instead
plant themselves in the hands of God?

They became trees that grant shade and stories
to anyone who would sit under them
and listen,
any who would come and picnic in their canopy
and stomach stories of pain buried in their bark.
If God would give me grace,
I would grow among them one day.
Faith would turn my feet into anchors,
root me deeply in a forest chorus
that would bid all those that walk by to
listen, to sit, to be seeds.

Bear Witness

When you were pregnant,
I watched you change.
I watched as your body
became more portal than person,
more passage than people.
I did my best to handle you with care.
As your steps slowed,
feet swole.
And, I wish I could say it completely happily,
I became a bellboy, cook, and chauffeur.
I was so arrogant then.
You see, I can only imagine what it is like
for my body to be stretched wide open like window
so a child that only existed in the imagination
of God can bleed through like wine on cloth.
I can only imagine what it is like to feel feet
kick your comfort, to never truly be alone,
to have the Holy Spirit mold soul in you.
God is the only one who can give life.
So, that must be why babies do not speak much;
they are still speechless from living in God's thoughts.
Children come from a place absent of time and full of the will of God.
The tenth month, the day of our anniversary, we went for a checkup.
In my heart, I faced the reality that I would have to face fatherhood soon.
How quickly fear becomes Pharaoh,
makes you its slave.
And then,
your water broke,
and God showed me how he can still use parting water to free
his people from a Pharaoh.
We both drowned in grace that day.
We had a birth plan as natural as possible.
I watched
each time as you grit your teeth during each contraction like
grindstone.
I watched

the wrinkles above your eye's labyrinth
as your thoughts searched for reason to give up and
found none.
You said you could take the pain if it had purpose.
You made it cathartic.
You were hungry.
They gave you ice chips,
which were as useful as watering the grass in the rain.
I felt the same way.
I felt like the ice chips,
broken and cold, sitting there,
watching the love of my life go through the pain of her life.
I felt helpless.
un-useful.
Wife,
my innate need to fix
to improve
to repair
are all worthless when it comes to birthing life.
I sat there quiet and convicted,
and no, there was not much I could do then.
But there was so much more I could have done
before.
Childbirth is a woman waging a war on the fortress of her body, and I
could have cared for the castle better, could've polished its halls with love
and patience.
I could have swept its stables with listening and dancing.
But, no, I let her king me,
sat on the throne of her heart heavy like iron.
I could have taken the trash out before the tone of the voice signified she
had told me before already.
I could let my character then
reinforce her for the war in her belly.
I love my wife.
I always have, but I have not been a good steward of her.
Have I not rehearsed her like poems?
So, husbands,
love your wife as Christ loved the church.

When her parties run out of wine.
Perform miracles for her.
When she thinks her two fish and five loaves of bread are not enough
prove God to her.
When she gives you her issues
crawl on your knees with her, reaching for the fullness in His hem.
My wife was in labor for 28 hours
until her body broke like alabaster,
revealing her beautifully bloody hallelujah.
I had no idea that becoming a father would make me more husband.
I have learned that a
woman's strength is remarkable.
I understand now why God will
always ask for labor before delivery,
for sowing before reaping,
for storms before peace.
Theo, our son, has changed my theology.

Sandcastles

It is both scary and humbling the moment when you realize your plans are but sandcastles to the ocean of His will.

Taser

Daunte Wright was killed during a traffic stop when the officer
thought she was pulling her taser but pulled her gun instead.
But
I get that she thought it was a taser.
It's fine.

Justice is blind anyway.
Well, colorblind anyway
By that I mean,
it only sees black and white.
She thought it was her taser,
she thought her life was in danger, Philando,
she thought it was her apartment, Botham Jean.
It seems that the most dangerous place for me isn't America,
it's in white imagination.

Ungrateful

Black self-love must seem so ungrateful.
Y'all went through all that trouble building stereotypes,
and we just mess around and disrobe.
Every morning, we dive into our skin with such dignity,
prove that black and beauty are not oxymoronic,
heads held high like church mothers on Sunday,
walk around dressed for God himself.
Y'all had recipes for us,
but we decided y'all didn't use enough seasoning.
So, we decided to slow cook a revolution in our chest,
and every year we taste better.
How dare we not stick to the script?
Be our multi layered, multi-colored selves?
Love our skin?
Blossoming such beauty comes natural when your skin
is the hue of soil.
Dang, they must feel so unappreciated
after y'all went through all that work casting us
in this grand play you call America.
Y'all sent slave ship Ubers to come and get us,
and some of my ancestors chose to tear up the script,
jump overboard.
How dare we sing so soulful atheists give an ovation?
Endure such sadness and come out on the other side?
And somewhere in the middle invent the Blues?
And mac and cheese?
Though you had choreography for us,
our bodies obey a beat that has been passed down from kin to kin.
Yea, it must seem so ungrateful.

Match Box

Marriages that have made unforgiveness a roommate
are nests built with match sticks:
one spark,
one text,
one lie,
and it will all burn,
and the birds that survive
all have singed wings, unable to fly.

Her Love

Her fingers waltz over my back,
prying,
hunting
for the brokenness.
When found,
she applies pressure,
searching for the fault lines in my soul,
a stress test of my spine.
She plays my ribs like piano,
shows me the value of the half notes.
I swear, she has turned our wedding bed
into an operating room.
Without warning, her eyes lash out,
make piñata out of my pride
until all my sweetness lay bare before her.
Her beauty forces submission.
Our relationship was a sour candy we both committed not to spit out.
Now we can both enjoy the sweet, sticky center.
My wife says my name like it is topping on ice cream.
No wonder I melt.
Especially on Sundaes.
My wife makes gravel out of my writer's block.
Her whispers are loaded guns.
She has robbed me of complaints,
of worry,
of self-doubt.
Her ambition was jet fuel that released me from
generational strongholds.
Her love laid siege to my procrastination.
She takes no prisoner but one,
me.
Her love is origami,
and, honestly,
I am molded by her love.
It hurts
to be bent, folded,

but I trust her when she says,
"I'm making something."

Black Fatherhood is a Rebellion

Sons,
according to stereotypes,
our every moment together is rebellious.
It is a waving flag,
a clenched fist.
It is proof that pigmentation and parenting
are not opposing forces.
Proof that the color of my skin
does not limit the depth of my love.
We turn playgrounds into protest.
Our laughter is hate speech to those
who would see us silent.
We turn tree lines at the park into picket signs.
We will show them
how contagious Black boy joy can be.
When you Rosa Parks my leg,
they want you to move from your seat.
I have learned to treat being a father as a sit-in.
And just like a tree,
we are here,
and we shall not be moved.
We shall not be moved.

Boomerang Prayers

Prayers are intended to be arrows:
knees bent as bow,
supplication a string.
But when prayers are hurled from hearts
that harbor hate,
when our quiver is full of those who we will never forgive,
they are cursed and curved,
never reaching the desired receiver.
They become boomerangs
pointing out our need to be prayed for ourselves.

Stereotypes

Stereotypes are dark magic
the way they make my identity disappear
like abracadabra, nothing up my sleeve,
in my mind,
in my heart.
Stereotypes are blind folds tied with ignorance and pride,
that camouflage you to truth
while, at the same time,
tipping the scales on your eyes.
The same pupils
that paint me weapon,
see me as threat,
will see a woman as damsel in distress.
Magical
how it will arm me
and
disarm her.
But I am not impervious.
I had a season
where I was sure that
rich meant evil
and white meant guilty.
Stereotypes always have the volume up
so we can't really hear each other.
They turn people to holsters for prejudice's
smoke and mirrors.
They do not just distort the truth,
they replace it with
Facebook posts,
Twitter feeds,
makes us think we know people we have never met,
fills our minds with half-truths,
makes Post-It notes out of life stories,
transforms the art of God into stick figures so
they fit in categories easier.
I wonder who decided how much diamonds were worth?

I wonder if they knew they were once carbon, once
black and dark
until stress gave it a new reflection.
Then
someone stole it from it soil habitat,
decided its value
because they believed it would look better in chains,
I mean,
better on chains.
I have seen,
we have seen this before.
They boarded boats,
sailed across the sea hungry for land.
Instead,
they found fields of people.
Their eyes never intended to land on such tones,
such hues;
men with skin like earth,
women with smiles as soft as Eden.
So, they snatched them from their habitat,
held up their lies like mirrors so they could not see their beauty anymore.
Told the women to only see themselves through the eyes of men.
They told them their skin was more stained than sculpture.
told men their history started when they were "found,"
that they could not be hands, just hammers.
Those syllables slithered into their psyche.
Now they fight,
read,
write,
advocate,
and
pray
to clean the lies from their lives,
to redeem their identities,
to rediscover an identity hidden in their DNA,
to be a diamond again.

Politics

Man's politics is a broken thing
It is a table with uneven legs
It is an unsure foundation
Unfit to hold up our hopes
It is stitched together with slimy promises
Forged with all the good intentions its slave owner founders could have
A place where people find allegiance to donkeys and elephants
Both arrogant and heavy
Both beasts bred of burden
Designed to carry a weight not their own
Neither willing to budge for the other
I watch as they fight
Play musical chairs in the White House
Their political house party sounds more like kids at play
Arguing whose turn it is to be team captain
And it's getting so hard to tell them apart
They wear suits and ties like swords and shields
all competing in a Game of Thrones
Making Lannister promises to their constituents
These knights in shining armor will dragon as soon as you let them
They will promise a torch for dark seasons
But their tongues will wildfire as they burn through billion-dollar budgets

Curious
They want me to separate the character of the country from its contents
That the label made in America should make me inspired
And not think of what is "in" America
Man's laws were never powerful enough to police the human heart
Man's laws are just scary enough to make men wear a civilian mask
Pay taxes and barbecue

I Lied to My Wife

I told my wife my gaze never wandered from her.
I told her each day my eyes swam upstream to her
to drink her in,
That every day my thirst was quenched in her.
I did not tell her the truth.
The truth is
at night I'd slip out of our vows like a loose garment
and put on shackles.
I would try to satisfy my flesh with salt water
when I was afraid, angry, or insecure.
I would try to drown my pain in fleeting pleasure.
My eyes lick forbidden fruit on websites,
bite down deep,
swallow the lie that sin
will keep its promise to satisfy.
The truth is there are lies
I still believe,
lies that drew me to computer screens,
to download satisfaction,
to see women like Play-Doh,
mold them into my fantasies.
When my wife was not looking,
I abandoned our family tree
and watered my secret rose bush
with time and affection
I vowed to give only to my wife.
My thoughts became a
Lil' shop of horrors,
a fly trap that
convinced me I needed to see more
until
one day
my wife found traces of what tempts me
in my un-erased history,
my dark habit dragged
into the light by its ankles.

I prepared for my destruction,
but when I looked at my wife,
her eyes
held a sad fire.
I had watered the tree I would hang from,
but she did not destroy me.
No arrow shaped accusations.
Her finger did not become laser pointers
to bring judgment to my brokenness.
She had no desire for blood.

She reached for me,
her hands dripping in prayer,
held me close.
Her love was a fire that burned my fig leaves.
She set out to wash my eyes with truth,
turned my view of God into a kaleidoscope
of grace and flesh.

That night,
I prayed like I never did before.
I learned
there is nothing like a guilty man's prayers.
They are brittle things,
a leak in the plumbing of my pride,
honest & naked.
The sweetest bliss
when your face is braced for fist,
but instead you feel a kiss.
This proves that there
is no difference between feeling loved and feeling safe.
When we allow ourselves to fall on the floor,
our cage is the only thing that breaks.

The Cost

Honesty was the most expensive choice I have ever made.

It has cost me:

> Friendships
> Relationships
> Stages
> Jobs
> Quiet

But now…

I can finally afford to be myself.

Eviction

When someone leaves your life
because you told them the truth,
they were in your life
for a lie.

Acknowledgments

I would like to express my deepest gratitude to my amazing wife, Victoria, who has been my unwavering pillar of support for the past nine years. Your incredible encouragement for both my mind and heart has been the driving force behind this book. Being loved well creates the safety for one to begin the journey of honesty. Thank you for not only standing by my side but also for watching over our children with love and care while I dedicated countless hours to its creation.

To my mother, whose boundless devotion to our family was evident in her indomitable spirit, I am eternally grateful. Your strength and love have been a constant source of inspiration throughout my life, and I dedicate this book to you.

I want to extend my heartfelt thanks to Pastor Jones, whose unwavering integrity has given me the courage to walk in character and bridge the gap between my ministry life and my personal life. Your guidance and wisdom have been instrumental in shaping the ideas within these pages.

To my friends, who have been there to hold my arms up when I was out of strength, who have engaged in countless conversations about random philosophical questions, and who have continued to love and support me despite it all–I couldn't have asked for better companions on this journey. Your friendship means the world to me.

Finally, I want to express my sincere gratitude to Camari Carter Hawkins, Founder of Mama's Kitchen Press. Your unwavering belief in me, coupled with your heart, passion, and patience, kept me from ever giving up on myself. Your dedication to nurturing voices like mine is a testament to your vision and commitment to the literary world.

Thank you all for being a part of this journey and for enriching my life in countless ways. Your support and encouragement have made this book possible, and for that, I am forever thankful.

Honestly,
Alexander James

About the Poet

Alexander James, is a man of many talents and accomplishments. He was born and raised in South LA and has used his experiences to become a successful poet, father, pastor, world traveler, and professional in his field.

As an Addy and Webby Award-winning poet, Alexander has made a name for himself in the creative world. He has also become a respected Poetry Coach, helping aspiring poets develop their skills and share their unique voices. Alexander has performed with some of the most renowned poets and speakers of our time, including Rudy Francisco, Propaganda, Derek Minor, and Dr. Cornel West. His talent and ability to connect with his audience have made him a sought-after performer and speaker.

As a father of four, Alexander has dedicated himself to providing for his family and being a positive influence in their lives. He takes great pride in his role as a parent and strives to be a loving and supportive figure for his children. In addition to his family and artistic pursuits, Alexander is also a pastor. He is deeply committed to his faith and uses his position to help others find comfort and guidance in their spiritual lives.

Alexander's love of travel has taken him to many corners of the world. He has explored different cultures and met people from all walks of life, gaining valuable insights and experiences along the way.

Connect with Alexander James at IAmAlexanderJames.com